A Congregation of Cows

Also by Robert Epstein:

A Walk around Spring Lake: Haiku

(Editor) Beyond the Grave: Contemporary Afterlife Haiku

(Editor) *The Breath of Surrender: A Collection of Recovery-Oriented Haiku*

Checkout Time is Noon: Death Awareness Haiku

Checkout Time is Soon: More Death Awareness Haiku

(Editor) Dreams Wander On: Contemporary Poems of Death Awareness

(Co-Editor with Miriam Wald) Every Chicken, Cow, Fish and Frog: Animal Rights Haiku

Haiku Days of Remembrance: In Honor of My Father

Free to Dance Forever: Mourning Haiku for My Mother

Haiku Edge: New & Selected Poems

Haiku Forest Afterlife

Healing into Haiku: On Illness and Pain

Nothing is Empty: A Whole Haiku World

(Editor) *Now This: Contemporary Poems of Beginnings, Renewals, and Firsts*

(With Stacy Taylor) *Suffering Buddha: The Zen Way Beyond Health and Illness*

(Editor) The Sacred in Contemporary Haiku

(Editor) The Temple Bell Stops: Contemporary Poems of Grief, Loss and Change

(Editor) They Gave Us Life: Mothers, Fathers & Others in Haiku

Turkey Heaven: Animal Rights Haiku

A Congregation of Cows:
Moo Haiku

By
Robert Epstein

Foreword by Nathaniel Altman
author of *The Nonviolent Revolution:
A Comprehensive Guide to Ahimsa*

*

Afterword by Miriam Wald, Ph.D.
activist and co-editor of *Every Chicken, Cow, Fish
and Frog: Animal Rights Haiku*

2019

ISBN 978-1-7335979-2-0

Middle Island Press
PO Box 354
West Union, WV 26456

Who are we to say that cats and dogs have more rights than cows and pigs?

~ Ellen de Generes

Cows are my passion. What I have ever sighed for is to retreat to a Swiss farm, and live entirely surrounded by cows. . .

~ Charles Dickens

Cow-slaughter and man-slaughter are in my opinion two sides of the same coin.

~ M. K. Gandhi

Eating liver out of a cow's body is like eating the filter out of a car.

~ Dick Gregory

A dead cow or sheep lying in a pasture is recognized as carrion. The same sort of a carcass dressed up and hung in a butcher's stall passes as food.

~ John Harvey Kellogg

The human body has no more need for cows' milk than it does for dogs' milk, horses' milk, or giraffes' milk.

~ Michael Klaper

I have a terrible image in my mind of a cow going to slaughter. . . . It's as if cows don't know that they have a choice. Not that they don't panic, but they do so in a quiet way.

~ Cloris Leachman

Real nutrition comes from soybeans, almonds, rice, and other healthy vegetable sources, not from a cow's udder.

~ Ingrid Newkirk

A mind of the caliber of mine cannot derive its nutrient from cows.

   ~ *George Bernard Shaw*

. . . I think the majority of cows, and even more so chickens and pigs, are leading pretty miserable lives.

   ~ *Peter Singer*

Cows scream louder than carrots.

   ~ *Alan Watts*

In Memory of:

Lyn Pock, Ph.D.

Michael G. Johnson, Jr.

Concetta Randazzo

Table of Contents

Acknowledgments

I wish to thank friends and family, including Janet Amptman, Kathy DiNapoli, Debbie Edwards, Clara Knopfler, Joy McCall, Sherry Phillips, Rocco Randazzo, Jay Schlesinger, Lillian Schwartz, Wendy Etsuku Siu, Sophie Soltani, Joan Vander Ryk. I am especially grateful to Stacy Taylor and Miriam Wald for their encouragement and input from beginning to end. A deep bow to Miriam for her editorial input and particularly for contributing her thoughtful and impassioned Afterword to the book.

I became an ethical vegan in July, 1975. Shortly after adopting a meatless diet, I found my way to a book by Nathaniel Altman, *Eating for Life: A Book about Vegetarianism*. It greatly helped guide me at the beginning of this undertaking, and I am eternally grateful to Nathaniel, which is why I asked him to contribute a Foreword to this book. It is my way of honoring his contribution to the vegan way of life I adopted 43 years ago.

In the Preface, I have included several cow-related haiku by other poets, because I find them moving and wanted to share a sampling of what other poets have written about cows. I greatly appreciate the permission each has granted to reprint their poems: Adrian Bouter, Alice Frampton, Peggy Heinrich, Deb Koen, Ron C. Moss, K. Ramesh, and Lynne Steel.

I am grateful to Christina Taylor of Middle Island Press for her outstanding help on yet another book project. Her kindness and attentiveness are much appreciated.

Foreword

A haiku is a Japanese poetic form that does not rhyme. It dates from the beginning of the Tokugawa Period 1600s, a time of political consolidation and great economic and cultural development. In Japanese tradition, a haiku consists of 17 syllables arranged in three lines containing five, seven, and five syllables, respectively. Known for its simplicity, a haiku can express both profound and powerful images and concepts in very few words.

Haiku remains Japan's most popular poetic form. Over the years, it has also become popular outside of Japan, and has been adapted in various degrees by poets who write in languages other than Japanese. As readers will see in Robert Epstein's *Congregation of Cows*, the haiku form serves as a powerful template for expressing essential ideas and images concerning our relationship with these noble animals.

Through Robert's poems, the reader can also perceive the essence of *ahimsa* – dynamic compassion – in compelling and elegant ways.

The teachings of dynamic compassion represent the essence of reverence for life to be applied in every facet of daily existence. Rather than an escape from the rough and tumble of the day-to-day world, ahimsa calls us to become deeply involved in life and its myriad challenges. Ahimsa is not a passive state of refraining from violence, but implies the active expression of compassion. It not only encompasses our philosophical attitudes towards war and peace, but directly impacts our daily interactions with family,

friends, colleagues and neighbors; the way we earn a living and how we spend our money; our relationship with the natural environment; how we view politics, business and education; and especially how we treat companion animals as well as domesticated animals used for food and leather, such as cows.

According to Gerald and Patricia Miche writing in *Toward a New World Order*, ahimsa is "an important concept not only in the development of a personal ecological ethic, but also as a philosophical foundation for the development of global structures that reinforce respect for, rather than violation of, the delicate balance and relatedness of all life forms." The true understanding of dynamic harmlessness encourages us to take personal responsibility to respect life and further it as much as possible.

According to Abraham Isaac Kook, one of the most celebrated rabbis of the twentieth century:

> With every moral improvement, with every good attribute, every worthwhile subject of study, every good deed, even the smallest, even a goodly conversation, one raises his own spiritual state; and

automatically when one part of existence rises to a higher state, all existence is uplifted.

By transforming our consciousness, we will help transform the consciousness of humanity. Even if five, ten or fifteen percent of the human population begins to dedicate ourselves towards practicing reverence for life and compassion towards other sentient beings in every aspect of our existence, a "cosmic shift" can occur in the minds and hearts of the rest of the human family. The simple verses in *A Congregation of Cows* inspire us to do this.

By working with small things from an inner place of truth, clarity and compassion, we can begin to reclaim our personal power, and play our part in transforming the world around us. Even though our efforts may never be recognized by others, the accumulated power of our individual thoughts, words and deeds can be considerable, and can help stem the tide of violence and cruelty in the world in favor of compassion and planetary healing. On a simple grassroots level, true personal empowerment can reflect the dynamic essence of ahimsa.

I feel privileged to contribute this Foreword to my friend Robert Epstein's *A Congregation of Cows*.

Nathaniel Altman
October 9, 2018

Preface

Cow protection is the gift of Hinduism
to the world.

~Mahatma Gandhi

Let me state passionately at the outset: This is *not* a book of haiku that perpetuates the fairytale of idyllic bliss for cows, which the factory farming industry has foisted upon unwitting carnivores and consumers of dairy and flesh for untold generations.

On the contrary, as a longtime vegan for spiritual and ethical reasons, I abhor the horrors and atrocities perpetrated against cows and calves (as well as countless pigs, sheep, chickens and other nonhumans). The limited time they may have on hills and in fields fenced in by barbed wire is no justification for their ultimate slaughter and dismemberment. While I do not ignore such atrocities, it is not my primary focus in these pages.

Instead, what I wish to do here is call attention to the wondrous lives of animals we call cows, to remind readers that they are *precious beings* with an existence independent of our own. Animals, fish and fowl are not here for the pleasure of our palate, nor were they created to serve humans in any way. The poet, Rainer

Maria Rilke, gives eloquent expression to the sensitivity and elevation of nonhuman beings quoted in *The Rilke Alphabet* (1):

> O how much truer are the animals
> that pace up and down in steel grids,
> unrelated to the antics of the new
> alien things which they don't understand. p.5

As Ulrich Baer puts it, Rilke regarded poetry as a means not only of understanding the world, but of revealing truths well-hidden by virtue of distorted beliefs and blind spots.

I couldn't agree more with the following assessment of Rilke's poetic life:

> Poetry becomes the record of the universe, and one of the words in this great and faithful transcription might reveal the universe's hidden meaning to us. The language of poetry does not turn away from the world towards a greater, transcendent Meaning but opens up to the world, and opens us *to* the immanence of the world, in which we live. ibid., p. x; italics in original

I am writing in these pages about the *suchness* of cows and calves, as my dear friend and animal rights activist, Miriam Wald, aptly terms it. Why? Because I am in awe of their sweetness and quiet majesty before their lives are brutally snuffed out at the slaughterhouse hidden in plain view.

What is *suchness?* The late haiku poet, Eric Amann, writing in *The Wordless Poem* (2), observes:

> . . . the haiku poet presents things "just as they are" – the "suchness of things." He gives us only the circumstances of an event, and of these only the barest minimum. "Touch and let go" is the secret of haiku art. p. 18

Admittedly, not all the poetry in these pages adheres faithfully to this core tenet. That is because I am deeply upset over the amount of suffering that bovines experience at the hands of human beings. I profoundly wish for radical change in our relationship to cows, calves and other nonhuman beings who suffer at the hands of humans.

Although I ardently maintain that one's relationship to nonhuman beings is a matter of individual conscience, I understand exactly what Zen and haiku scholar, R. H. Blyth, intends in the passage below:

> True Zen then must make people not hate animals, not wish to kill them, not rejoice in their violent or natural death. It must make one wish to reduce as much as possible the unnecessary, that is, the meaningless, that is, the Zen-less, the unpoetical suffering in the world. To put the matter in an extreme form, *no man [or woman] has true Zen in him, no man has true satori, that is, poetry, who is not, or does not*

become, a vegetarian. (3); emphasis added

Cows and Cow Protection in India

In the Hindu religious tradition, which dates back thousands of years, cows have been singled out for reverence and protection since ancient times. As Steven Rosen points out in *Food for the Spirit: Vegetarianism and the World Religions* (4): "Of all creatures, the cow is given a special place in the Indian religious traditions." p. 93. The *Vedas*, the voluminous body of scriptures in Hinduism, contain numerous references to the sacredness of cows. As Rosen summarizes:

> Traditionally, the cow is also considered dear to Lord Krishna, Who is glorified in the *Vedas* as the Supreme Lord. Vaishnavism, or the worship of Vishnu or Krishna, is the original religion of the *Vedas*, and Krishna's love for the cow is celebrated throughout the Vedic texts. It is no wonder, therefore, that we find a great emphasis on *ahimsa* and especially cow protection in the earliest parts of the Vedic literature. p. 93

Ahimsa is a Sanskrit word that means nonviolence or non-harming. Rosen highlights the connection between the practice of Hinduism and *ahimsa* in the following passage:

Ahimsa loosely translates as "nonviolence." In the Vedic tradition, however, the word possesses a much broader meaning: "Having no ill will for any living being, in all manners possible and for all times is called *ahimsa*, and it should be the desired goal of all seekers." (*Patanjali Yoga Sutras*, 2:30). p. 72

It is not hard to see how *ahimsa* translates into actively safeguarding the well-being of cows as well as all other living beings. Mahatma Gandhi was moved by the spirit of *ahimsa* to initiate a crusade to provide greater political and religious protection of bovines in India. Referring to the bovine as "Mother cow," Gandhi maintained that, by virtue of their many "selfless gifts" to humans, bovines should be regarded with the same reverence (if not more) as human mothers. (5) Thus, many Hindus engage in cow worship as well as vegetarianism in accordance with the Vedic teaching of *ahimsa*, as Rosen notes:

> The large number of Hindu vegetarians can be attributed, in great measure, to the very clear teaching of universal compassion found in the Vedic literature. Acknowledging two distinct levels of ethical consideration, the Vedas promote *sarva-bhuta-hita* ("devotion to the good of all creatures") over *loka-hita* ("devotion to the good of humanity"). The first ethical system, say the Vedas, includes the second. If one cares for

all living creatures, then one naturally cares for humanity, as well. p. 93

From my vantage point, the spiritual imperative at the heart of the Vedic teaching on *ahimsa* transcends a utilitarian view of cows as sacred by virtue of what they offer humans in the form of milk, curd, ghee, urine, and fertilizer. Janet Barkas, writing in *The Vegetable Passion: A History of the Vegetarian State of Mind*, echoes this point: Many Hindus "feel that the sacred cow developed because of a high regard for milk as a food for babies: forbidding the killing of cows ensured the continuation of a milk supply." p. 27 However, I passionately maintain that cows—*and all beings*—should be equally regarded with reverence and compassion as precious incarnations, rather than as commodities. This is the essence of a vegan—more so than a vegetarian—way of life; it is veganism that represents the fulfillment of our intimate relationship with Nature and all beings within it.

Conclusion

I am far from alone in experiencing wonder and awe evoked by the cows and calves in our lives. A number of other haiku poets have been similarly moved to write about their encounters with bovines, both young and old. Here is a sampling drawn from the anthology that Miriam Wald and I edited, *Every Chicken, Cow, Fish and Frog: Animal Rights Haiku*.

I will let the poems, written with great sensitivity, speak for themselves. May they too touch your heart as they have mine.

postmortem
the cow busy licking
her calf alive

~*Adrian Bouter*

dead calf
a mother licks
the wind

~*Alice Frampton*

footsteps on gravel
every cow
turns and stares

~*Peggy Heinrich*

Farm Sanctuary
friends
we didn't eat

~*Deb Koen*

white dawn ...
the calve's breath
on the udder

~ Ron C. Moss (6)

old milkers
their trail of cow pats
lit by the moon

~ Ron C. Moss

sunlit valley ...
the little shepherdess talks
to a calf

~ K. Ramesh

spring grass
I tell the calf
I'm a vegetarian

~ Lynne Steel

Notes

1. U. Baer, *The Rilke Alphabet*. A. Hamilton, tr. New York, NY: Fordham University Press, 2014.

2. E. W. Amann, *The Wordless Poem: A Study of Zen in Haiku*. Toronto, Canada: The Haiku Society of Canada, 1978.

3. R. H. Blyth, *Zen and Zen Classics*, vol. 7. New York, NY: Hokuseido Press, 1962; p. 58.

4. S. Rosen, *Food for the Spirit: Vegetarianism and the World Religions*. New York, NY: Bala Books, 1987.

5. Ibid. p. 93.

6. *The Heron's Nest*, 9, 2007.

Robert Epstein
El Cerrito, CA
6 January 2019

Poems

Passing Cows

passing cows
on the way
to a vegan meal (1)

the cows pay us no mind
humans whizzing by
on our way to nowhere

grazing cows
a stone's throw
from Muir's home (2)

lone shrub oak
far from useless
to the cows

who would've thought
Bashō's little white flower
among these cows

a worried man
with a worried mind
stopped in his tracks

~ *after Bob Dylan*

roadside cross
what the cows
can't say

their fate aside
I envy the cows so far
from our urban blight

not exactly
tiptoeing through
a sunflower field

legs folded under them
how innocent they look
lying in the sun

why do I
see snow where there is none
black & white cows

freeway drive
if I could, I would join
the congregation of cows

How They Are

what of the bay can the cows hear?

hillside grazing
they could teach hoofers
a thing or two

with no thought
of the morrow, she drops
a cow pod

wind picks up
        so do the cows

back again
the cow that jumped
over the moon

sweet grass
a newborn calf
nuzzling her mother

such tenderness large numbers lying in the grass

I would sooner
count on these kinfolk
than some of my neighbors

around them
a family of gophers
with little to fear

the way
summer grass yields
to the cows
in song

trying to determine
which of the cows
kicked the bucket

daily headlines
how often do you hear. . .
cow violence

one more cow skull
willed back
to the Earth

Hidden in Plain View

bobble-head cow
if the bank teller
only knew

so much land
as far as the eye can see
not a single bull

long summer day
cows roaming mostly free
the pesticides

what crows know
but cows can't hear
calves gone missing

killing it, *absolutely not*

~ *in protest of Camas Davis (3)*

circling hawks
because of your cravings
they can't come home

hidden in the hills
Holstein dairy cows
locked to a trough

spilled
milk
I
cry
over
the
cow

unseen here
nose rings   in calves
still needing   to nurse (4)

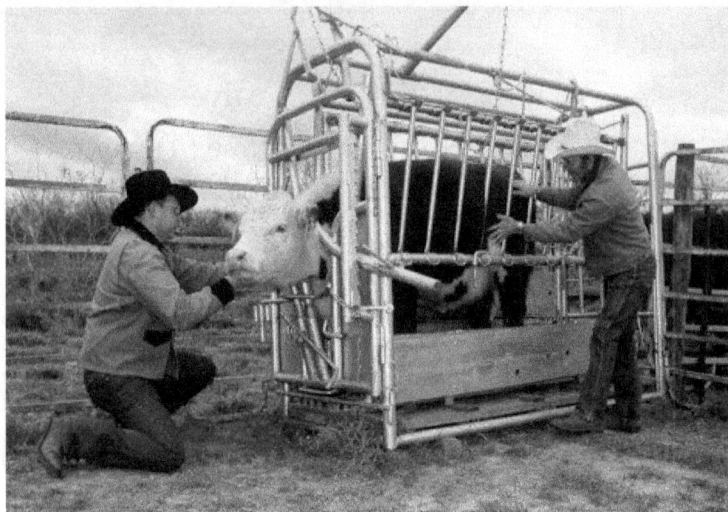

caged. . .
how kind of "researchers"
to look for ticks

herd mentality—
who's at the heart
of it here?

wolf moon
not a single one knows
what awaits them

coyote alert. . .
the cattle rancher cares
let's call it *profit*

what's a *slaughter tag*, mommy?

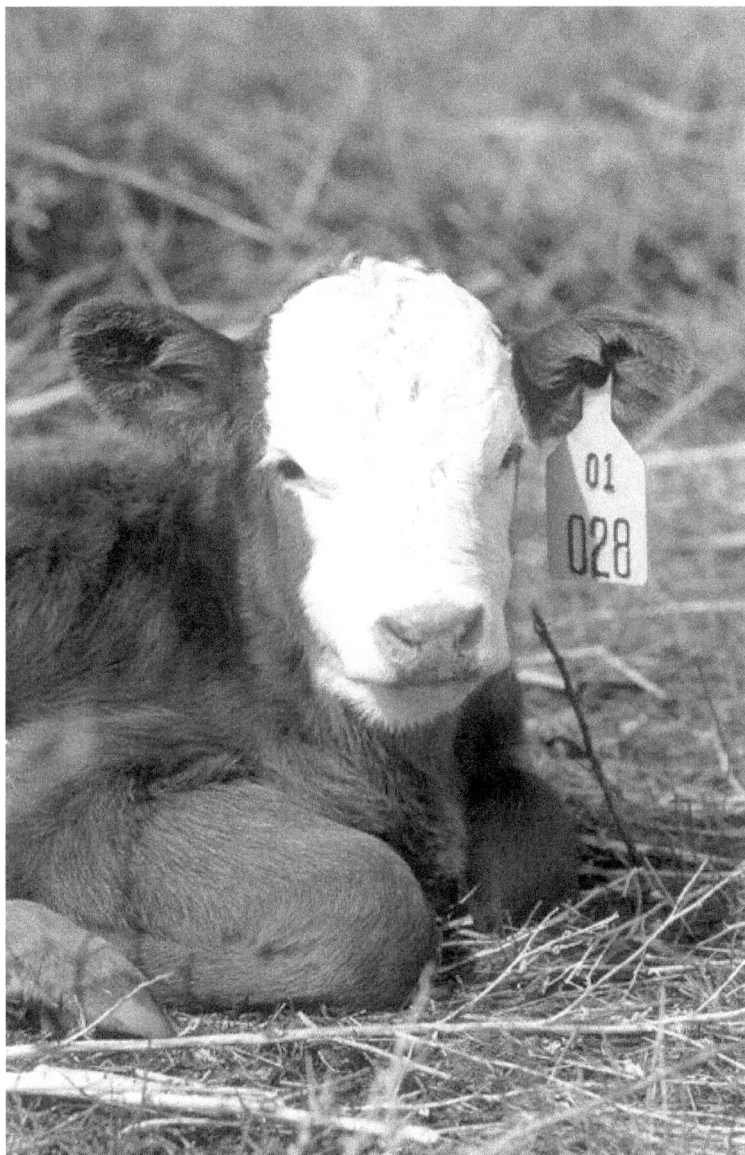

pray tell the difference
between what the ranchers do
& the Nazis' did

how that road
on the range stops
at the slaughterhouse

that silent train
over the rusted trestle
to or from Auschwitz?

not for milking, *not* for meat

setting sun
and so too
another's life

real cows
not cartoons
get slaughtered

Like Them, Like Us

the true heart
of a cow as distant to me
as the floating moon

back in bed
after a midnight snack
my tummy mooing too

long summer sunday
I recognize
her yawn

Mozart, Brahms
the music cows make
swishing tails

downpour—
how the cows know
to huddle too

mostly grass
I wish I too could be
that kind of vegan

a heifer depends on water too

others hang back
who is that marked cow
staring me in the eye

if you harm her, you harm me

unknowing their fate
they amble, graze, doze and play
like you or me

make no mistake
they too desire
what you & I do

Aghyna

in these hills
there is no golden calf
flesh-and-blood is all

between heaven & earth
an untroubled Holstein
stands alone

it's a low moo
still she reaches them
across the miles

her face, her gaze
that one could be
my mother now

a peaceful end. . .
your children deserve it
so do hers

single file the way to peace

what would cows do
if they were free. . .
follow the moo

in that other world moo means *mu (6)*

open book—
I know why the Hindus
see them as holy

no need to smear
my body with secretions
beholding them is enough

the mystery behind those eyes

I close my eyes
all the barbed wire is gone
and so are cows

the answer
in flesh and blood
yes

Notes

1. In the summer of 1975, I was confronted by a self-styled vegetarian (who hid anchovies in her pantry) about my meat eating, which I had never questioned. This casual confrontation ultimately led to my decision to adopt a vegan way of life. I gave up all meat, fish, and fowl as well as animal by-products, including honey, eggs, dairy, and leather—to name a few. For me, veganism is much more than a dietary regimen; it is, as I have said, *a way of life*. Even if I learned that my health has been compromised by living as a vegan, I would adhere to it, come what may.

2. John Muir (1838-1914) wrote eloquently on behalf of Nature and helped to establish the National Park System during President Theodore Roosevelt's term in office. His home in Martinez, CA is now a historical site that is open to the public.

3. Camas Davis is a "meat activist" who went to France to study "whole animal butchery." Her book, *Killing It: An Education,* is part of a recent movement for "meat education and reform," which includes the "Good Meat Project"— a program she founded that purports to promote "responsible" meat production and consumption.

Every fiber in my body and soul revolts against what Davis and others like her are doing. Why? Because I know in depth of my heart that meat-eating is utterly unnecessary for human survival. I regard the violence against animals that Davis is promoting as regressive and reactionary in terms of the advancement of civilization rooted in compassion and respect for all, including nonhuman beings.

4. A rancher forces a large steel ring into a calf's nose to prevent the calf from nursing and thereby depleting her mother's milk, which is then exploited for commercial purposes.

5. *Aghyna* is a Sanskrit word appearing in the Rigveda (circa: 1200-1500 BCE)—one of India's sacred texts—which refers to milk cows as those who "may not be slaughtered."

6. *Mu* is an important word in Zen Buddhism and a response to a famous koan or riddle in which a Zen monk asked Zen teacher, Joshu: "Does a dog have buddha-nature?" Joshu responded: "Mu," which means "no" or "not have," "without." *Mu* could also be interpreted as "not applicable" insofar as a dualistic way of thinking (yes versus no) is wholly inadequate in terms of Self-realization or enlightenment.

Afterword

The Rabbit, the Apple, and the Child

There is a thought-provoking vignette that beautifully illustrates our inborn tendency towards non-harming:

If a rabbit and an apple are placed into a child's crib, what happens?

Most likely, the child will reach out to stroke the rabbit and eat the apple, rather than the other way around. It is this very impulse—to behold gently, rather than to cause harm—that we humans have to *unlearn* in order to participate in our predominantly animal-eating culture.

Each "moo haiku" in these pages has offered the opportunity to reclaim our birthright—our innate, compassionate tendencies:

such tenderness large numbers lying in the grass

*

downpour
how the cows know
to huddle too

*

no need to
smear my body with secretions
beholding them is enough

These cow-inspired haiku help us reveal to ourselves who *we* really are, just as we get to see who *they* really are. We are invited, *in this very moment*, to undo a lifetime of conditioning when we read and experience these poems.

Miriam Wald
Santa Rosa, CA
December 29, 2018

Recommended Reading

Altman, N., *Eating for Life: A Book About Vegetarianism.* Wheaton, IL: Quest, 1973.

_____. The *Nonviolent Revolution: A Comprehensive Guide to Ahimsa – The Philosophy and Practice of Dynamic Harmlessness.* n/p: Gaupo Publishing, 2017.

Barkas, J. *The Vegetable Passion: A History of the Vegetarian State of Mind.* NY: Charles Scribner's Sons, 1975.

Bekoff, M. *The Animal Manifesto: Six Reasons for Expanding Our Compassion Footprint.* Novato: New World Library, 2007.

_____. *Animals Matter: A Biologist Explains Why We Should Treat Animals with Compassion and Respect.* Boston: Shambhala, 2007.

Braunstein, M. M. *Radical Vegetarianism.* Los Angeles: Panjandrum Books, 1983.

Burnett, G. *The Vegan Book of Permaculture: Recipes for Healthy Eating and Earthright Living.* White River Junction, VT: Chelsea Green Publishing, 2015.

Carson, G. Men, *Beasts, and Gods: A History of Cruelty and Kindness to Animals.* NY: Charles Scribner's Sons, 1972.

Davis, B. and Vesanto, M. *Becoming Vegan: The Complete Guide to Adopting a Healthy Plant-Based Diet*. Book Publishing, 2000.

Dinshah, F. *The Vegan Kitchen*. Malaga, NJ: American Vegan Society, 1965.

Dinshah, H. J. and Dinshah, A. *Powerful Vegan Messages*. Malaga, NJ: American Vegan Society, 2014.

Dombrowski, D. A. *The Philosophy of Vegetarianism*. Amherst: The University of Massachusetts Press, 1984.

Epstein, R. *Turkey Heaven: Animal Rights Haiku*. West Union, WV: Middle Island Press, 2016.

Epstein, R. and Wald, M., eds. *Every Chicken, Cow, Fish and Frog: Animal Rights Haiku*. West Union, WV: Middle Island Press, 2016.

Giehl, D. *Vegetarianism: A Way of Life*. NY: Harper & Row, 1979.

Harris, M. "India's Sacred Cow." *Human Nature*, 1978,18, pp. 200-210.

Jha, D. N. *The Myth of the Holy Cow*. New York, NY: Verso, 2002.

Klaper, M. *Vegan Nutrition: Pure and Simple*. Kapaau, HI: Gentle World, Inc., 1997.

Mason, J. and Singer, P. *Animal Factories*. NY: Crown Publishers, 1980.

Moran, V. *Compassion: The Ultimate Ethic.* Wellingborough, Northhamponshire: Thorsons Publishers, 1985.

Phelps, N. *The Great Compassion: Buddhism and Animal Rights.* NY: Lantern Books, 2004.

Primack, G. *Kind Poems.* Woodstock, NY: Post Traumatic Press, 2013.

Regan, T. *All That Dwell Therein: Essays on Animal Rights and Environmental Ethics.* Berkeley: University of CA Press, 1982.

_____. *The Case for Animal Rights.* Berkeley: University of CA Press, 1983.

Regan, T. and Singer, P., eds. *Animal Rights and Human Obligations.* Englewood Cliffs, NJ: Prentice-Hall, 1976.

Rollin, B. E. *Animal Rights and Human Morality.* Buffalo, NY: Prometheus Books, 1981.

Rosen, S. *Food for the Spirit: Vegetarianism and the World Religions.* NY: Bala Books, 1987.

Salt, H. *Animals' Rights: Considered in Relation to Social Progress.* Clarks Summit, PA: Society for Animal Rights, 1980.

Singer, P. *Animal Liberation.* NY: Avon, 1977.

_____, ed. *In Defense of Animals*. NY: Basil Blackwell, 1985.

Sure, H., ed. *Kindness: A Vegetarian Poetry Anthology*. Burlingame, CA: Dharma Realm Buddhist Association, 2010.

Winston, K. "The Splainer: What Makes the Cow Sacred to Hindus?" *Washington Post*, November 5, 2015.

Wise, S. M. *Drawing the Line: Science and the Case for Animal Rights*. NY: Perseus Books, 2002.

_____. *Rattling the Cage: Toward Legal Rights of Animals*. NY: Perseus Books, 2000.